Not love perhaps...

poems by

A S J Tessimond

selected and introduced by HUBERT NICHOLSON

AUTOLYCUS PUBLICATIONS 14 Barlby Road London W10 6AR

ISBN 0 903413 18 3

CONTENTS

ERRATA

Page 22: line one should read
'I am the city of two divided cities'

Page 27: line one should read
'He finds that talk of music, books and art is'

INTRODUCTION

In a sense, Arthur Seymour John Tessimond (1902-1962) was born and died before his time. The longing he so constantly expressed in his poems for an 'unperplexed, unvexed time,' for a 'one day' when 'people will touch and talk perhaps easily' and will 'unfurl, uncurl like seaweed returned to the sea', chimes prophetically with the hopes and desires of a younger generation today.

In another way he was very much of his time. That distinctly old-fashioned type, a heterosexual bachelor, he had something of the man-about-town in his makeup: an elegant, fair, mannerly figure, at large with rolled umbrella in the big-city streets, keen-eyed but uncynical, equipped with tolerance and humour and humility, as his poems bear witness. He had a most engaging candour and simplicity, but sought to 'offer no angles to the wind', as he says of his cats.

Although I knew and admired John's verse before I knew and loved the man, I can scarcely hope to be an impartial judge. We were friends with never a coolness for over twenty years, and his will named me his literary executor. In that capacity I have observed a strange phenomenon.

During his lifetime he was tolerably well known and becoming more so. He contributed to many publications on both sides of the Atlantic. He was one of that notable group in Michael Roberts's *New Signatures* (1934), in which Auden, Spender and Day Lewis made their mark The British Council taped him reading his own work. He published three books of verse, the third being a Poetry Book Society choice. In literary gossip he was an 'OK name'.

Then, after his sudden death in his Chelsea flat from a brain haemorrhage, a silence seemed to fall. His books were out of print. Unjust neglect seemed to be leading to the dark tower of oblivion.

I say 'seemed' because I, and perhaps I alone, knew otherwise. More and more often I was asked to give permission to reprint Tessimond poems in anthologies and schoolbooks, quote them in examination papers, recite them from platforms, use them as verse-speaking test-pieces, and broadcast them now and then in Britain, Canada, Africa, Australia and New Zealand. To mention a single instance, 'The Man in the Bowler Hat' has been requested eleven times in the last four years.

The reason for his appeal to children and their teachers lies less in his subjects than in the absolute lucidity of his verse. He was indefatigable in listening to and looking at his poems, rethinking, tuning and polishing, never afraid of losing spontaneity in the process, believing like Dr. Johnson that everything he had written could be improved by being worked over once more. I am not sure the final form was always the best, but it was always the clearest.

Now at last this so to speak submerged talent has broken surface again. The point of real emergence was the radio programme 'Portrait of a Romantic' by H Colin Davis, which put the poetry in the context of the character. There was an excellent public response, which led to a repeat. It included readings of fourteen poems, the title one being from the tape of the author's voice, and a discerning commentary. Mr Davis was perfectly justified in taking the title poem to be a self-portrait, although I would suggest it painted only one aspect. Tessimond was standing well back from himself — there is irony in the last line, 'He tries to climb the wall around the world', for he was an anti-romantic as well as a romantic.

He called his first book *The Walls of Glass,* from lines in his 'Nursery Rhyme for a 21st Birthday.' This image had a double significance for him. It stood for what he felt was wrong with our social life, its artificialities and false relationships, its unacknowledged barriers — 'glass is nothing until you try to pass it' — and it came from his private psychological frustrations and fears — 'for glass will break you even while you break it.' Hence the poignancy of his poetry of never-quite-fulfilled love. One thinks of Shelley's saying about the poets: 'They learn in suffering what they teach in song.' Although I see John as greatly enjoying life in his best years, he did suffer. Two years of psychoanalysis in his thirties failed to help him, merely telling him what he already knew, that he felt deprived of maternal love in his childhood. In later years he became manic-depressive and underwent frequent electric shock treatment, which may have shortened his life, but equally may have averted a suicide that in dark times seemed inevitable. One cannot know. But through his walls of glass he, as eternal spectator, saw the world very sharply. Lookers-on see most of the game, which helps to account for his astute delineation of modern archetypes, and his acute ear for the tones and overtones of the 'voices in a giant city.'

John always professed to hate 'cultural events' and literary parties, but he went to a good many and was more sociable than he admitted. He was one of the first members of a poetry-reading circle (still active) which I and others founded in Epsom in 1950, and used to read his new work there. He even read parts in its theatricals, once impersonating Coleridge as Mr Flosky in *Nightmare Abbey.* It was at a party before the Second World War that he and I first met, in the Bloomsbury flat of Roger Roughton, surrealist and editor of the little magazine *Contemporary Poetry and Prose.* Quite a party, seeing that the guests included James Thurber, e e cummings, William Empson, Arthur Calder-Marshall, Ruthven Todd and Nina Hamnett. But it was three years later that John came across a description of it in a book of mine (*Half my Days and Nights*) and wrote enthusiastically, suggesting we meet again. His letter said 'I got a great kick out of this first and probably last time of meeting my name in a book, other than one or two books on present-day verse.' A couple of weeks later he visited me and my family in the Midlands. Meantime I had asked him about himself and had received a characteristic self-appraisal, which he called 'an egoist's picnic.' He said he was thirty-nine, lived in Bayswater, was employed by Glaxo writing ads, was 'a lazy reader,' and had psychological troubles.

He then set out the things he liked, 'from which you can deduce something or other, probably.' It was a very long list, covering films (from *Le Million* and *Potemkin* to *His Girl Friday* and the Marx Brothers); singers (from Charles Trenet to Marlene Dietrich); books (Baudelaire, R C Hutchinson, Housman, Marvell, Rupert Brooke . . .); painters (Modigliani, El Greco, 'Picasso's drawings of women with big toes'. . .); food and drink (marmalade, kippers, Pimms No.1, vin ordinaire, Gentleman's Relish); places (Paris, London, Cumberland, and 'daydreams of the South Sea Islands as they probably aren't and perhaps never were'); and people, including 'cuties with small noses and full mouths and rather babyish voices and blue eyelids; quadroon and octoroon girls'. Among his favourite occupations he mentioned: 'Getting to know girls in the choruses of revues by writing them notes and arranging to meet them Saturday noon at Oddenino's.'

Those girls, and his models and dance-hostesses and strippers, were perhaps more often gold-diggers than poetry-lovers, but some were kind-hearted and one or two became true friends. He flattered them, took them abroad, showered presents and poems on them – some wrote bits of verse in return. But his eye wasn't entirely clouded by his adoration. Once when he was rhapsodising about the latest goddess, I asked what she looked like. He thought a moment and then replied seriously 'I think she looks rather like a female prize-fighter.'

Summing up his life in one of his early letters to me, he said: 'I had a middle-class provincial adolescence' (his father was a bank inspector.) 'Lived in Birkenhead till I was 14; then two years at Charterhouse; then I refused to go back to school and ran away to London and planned to earn my living as a free-lance journalist, but hadn't the guts to try for more than a fortnight, after which time I let myself be trotted back to Birkenhead. Then a year doing nothing particular, then four years at Liverpool University, during which I got engaged to a girl who was morbidly afraid of having a child. Then two terms of teaching. Then a year and a half working in London bookshops. And finally copywriting . . . Politics? Socialist' – adding, however, that he had 'practically no social sense,' a statement to which his verse gives the lie.

When war came, he determined not to go into the forces, an unconscientious objector. 'I should be not only intensely miserable but bloody well useless and even dangerous to others as a soldier,' he wrote. So he threw up his job, left his flat, tried to live from hand to mouth, undetected, and became intensely miserable. At length he submitted to his medical and was promptly rejected as unfit. Tragi-comedies of this kind were his lot, and he saw their humour. Once, attracted by a gorgeous girl on a travel poster, he rushed off to Jamaica hoping to find her equal ('his Jumbly girl' as Mr Davis says.) He didn't, and fell ill. Local doctors diagnosed advanced tuberculosis and he hurried back to London to see a specialist. Verdict: a common cold. But the trip at least produced his poem, 'Jamaican Bus Ride.'

He exhibits skill in many poetic forms, from free verse to the heroic couplet. A critic has said that in 'Black Monday Lovesong' he is the first poet since Longfellow to dare to use the metre of 'Hiawatha' (trochaic dimeters) for a serious poem. He can be witty and even ferocious, as in his posthumously-published attack on his profession, 'The Ad-man'. (A sense of fairness made him attempt a counter-balancing defence, with the rather dubious contention that 'Coloured water sometimes can assuage/A thirst for draughts from unattainable wells.') His best-known poem, 'Cats', is as shapely as its subject. One of a pair of cat poems in his first book, it matches with the earlier 'Night Life' and the three can be compared here. The last-named was one of scores of poems retrieved from old magazines by the tireless researches of Mrs Jean Cooper, to whom this volume is accordingly much indebted. Outstanding among hitherto uncollected poems is 'Heaven' (1962), since broadcast in BBC TV's 'Closedown', as well as in Mr Davis's programme.

This collection is not chronological. Once Tessimond had shed the excessive early influence of Pound, Eliot and the Imagists, he was not a poet of much development. I have grouped the poems in three sections – roughly: (I) poems about love; (II) contemporary types and situations; and (III) impressions and meditations.

Preferences will differ, but I believe the cream of his work is here: the essence of a true and truthful poet, the vision of a sensitive and open-hearted man.

A S J Tessimond's three books of verse were:

The Walls of Glass (Methuen, 1934)
Voices in a Giant City (Heinemann, 1947)
Selection (Putnam, 1958)

Poems in the present volume not included in those books first appeared in *The Listener, New Statesman, Times Literary Supplement, Adelphi, New Coterie* and *This Quarter,* to whose publishers, and to the *New Yorker* ('A Hot Day'), acknowledgment is due.

My thanks for most helpful advice are due to four people who knew the poet well: Peter and Kit Stanford, and Dawson Jackson and his wife (Joan Hart).

Hubert Nicholson

A S J Tessimond

I

NOT LOVE PERHAPS

This is not Love perhaps – Love that lays down
Its life, that many waters cannot quench, nor the floods
drown –
But something written in lighter ink, said in a lower tone:
Something perhaps especially our own:
A need at times to be together and talk–
And then the finding we can walk
More firmly through dark narrow places
And meet more easily nightmare faces:
A need to reach out sometimes hand to hand–
And then find Earth less like an alien land:
A need for alliance to defeat
The whisperers at the corner of the street:
A need for inns on roads, islands in seas, halts for discoveries to be shared,
Maps checked and notes compared:
A need at times of each for each
Direct as the need of throat and tongue for speech.

BLACK MONDAY LOVESONG

In love's dances, in love's dances
One retreats and one advances.
One grows warmer and one colder,
One more hesitant, one bolder.
One gives what the other needed
Once, or will need, now unheeded.
One is clenched, compact, ingrowing
While the other's melting, flowing.
One is smiling and concealing
While the other's asking, kneeling.
One is arguing or sleeping
While the other's weeping, weeping.

And the question finds no answer
And the tune misleads the dancer
And the lost look finds no other
And the lost hand finds no brother
And the word is left unspoken
Till the theme and thread are broken.

When shall these divisions alter?
Echo's answer seems to falter:
'Oh the unperplexed, unvexed time
Next time . . . one day . . . one day . . . next time!'

THE ADVISERS

Reason says, 'Love a girl who does not love you?
  Learn to forget her, learn to let her go!'
But Fate says, 'When I sent you far to find her
  I had a plan whose end you cannot know.'

Reason says, 'Love like this will bring you a thousand
  Unhappy days for every happy hour.'
'To give great joy,' says Fate; 'without great suffering,
  Light without shadow, lies beyond my power.'

'Can you,' says Reason, 'love a girl in love with
  Another man? Have you no pride, no will?'
'I am using you,' says Fate; 'have faith; be humble.
  Tools are not told what purpose they fulfil.'

'What she needs,' Reason says, 'you cannot give her,
  Nor she what you need.' 'No, not now,' says Fate;
'But both of you will change. When you are ready
  To play your parts, you will. Be patient. Wait.'

Reason says, 'If you chase a dream through darkness,
  What but confusion, misery can you find?'
Fate says, 'Before you lies a long hard journey,
  But I can see the way though you are blind.'

Reason says, 'Look, there are easier paths to choose from
  And lesser goals with greater hopes of gain.'
But Fate says, 'You are the chosen, not the chooser.
  I give you, friend, the privilege of pain.'

MIDDLE-AGED CONVERSATION

'Are you sad to think how often
You have let all wisdom go
For a crimson mouth and rounded
Thighs and eyes you drowned in?' 'No.'

'Do you find this level country,
Where the winds more gently blow,
Better than the summit raptures
And the deep-sea sorrows?' 'No '

CONVERSATION WITH MYSELF

'Lie down, heart. Do not run to meet her. See,
The path is clear and who can come but she?
Rest now, let be.
When two, as you and she, agree
To laugh at time, they're timeless, free.
Let go. Let be.

Let be; here's none but you and she and fate.
Your world's without dimension, distance, date;
And all things come, fool heart, to those who wait.'
'No, no. Love has dimension, distance, date;
And all things come perhaps to those who wait . . .
But some too late.'

LOVERS' CONVERSATION

'Why do we hurt each other,
We two, so much and often?
Why does the heart so quickly
Harden and slowly soften?'

'Love itself hurts the lover
Who sighs and cries for release
From the joy that is partly sorrow
And the passion that's never peace.'

THE BARGAIN

Love hurt you once, you said, too much.
You said you'd have no more of such
Hot heartbreak and long loneliness.
You said you'd give and ask for less
Than love, that daemon without pity,
That far, miraged, red, golden city
Across the desert of desire,
Ringed with the gateless ring of fire.

You said you'd drink, but not too deep,
Of life: explore yet always keep
Your final secret self intact,
Entire, untied, untorn, unracked.

And I, may heaven forgive me, said,
'Lay your blonde beloved head
In the hollow of my arm:
We'll love lightly without harm
To either's heart; and I'll defy
Your warmth and loveliness; and I
Won't love too much'.
Forgive my lie!

TWO MEN IN A DANCE HALL

Tom laughs, is free and easy;
And girls obey his call,
For whether they obey it
He hardly cares at all.

But Edward burns with longing;
And angry anxious pain
Cries from his eyes too loudly,
Too eagerly, in vain.

THE TOO MUCH LOVED

It has been written in your star
That fire shall kindle where you are:
That where you walk there shall be strife;
Ice melting; earth turned; sleep stirred; life.

You will graze hearts and blood will spurt,
You will be hurt because you hurt
Those whom you try not even to touch,
Whose eyes pursue your eyes too much.

You will bring peace but oftener still
Wars in your name against your will;
Yet you divider, waker of
Angers will suffer too much love.

And you will stir the whirlpool up,
And you will drink the unasked for cup,
And be of those much damned and blessed
Who never rest, who never rest.

AFTER ATTEMPTED ESCAPE FROM LOVE

He who has once been caught in a silver chain may burn
and toss and fret.
He will never be bound with bronze again; he will not
be forgiven; will never forget.
He who has eaten the golden grapes of the sun will call
no sour fruit sweet.
He will turn from the moon's green apples and run,
though they fall in his hand, though they lie at his
feet.

SONG

A year ago, I was saying,
' I must be free as air
To turn at any street-corner
And stop on any stair
And follow the shadow of any eyelash,
The flare of passing hair. '

To-day, I find myself saying,
' I need north-south; a pole;
Lodestone and fixed abode, now;
Compass; a map; control;
Something less cold than the fugitive eye;
Not part of love, but the whole. '

Is it the end of youth, then
(Youth not young unless wild)?
Or is it the slow beginning
Of ceasing to be a child
Playing with bricks or the sun in water;
Half-born, self-beguiled?

POSTSCRIPT TO A PETTINESS

Though you'll forgive (I think, my sweet)
My larger sins of haste and heat
And lust and fear, can you forgive
My inabilities to live?
Can you despise me not too much
When most I lack the human touch,
And keep no date, no diary of
Days when I fail, dear love, to love?

ACKNOWLEDGEMENT

When I was lonely
Your fingers reached for mine, their touch
Natural as sunlight's.

When I was hardened
Your warmness thawed my rock as gently
As music thought.

When I was angry
You smiled: 'But this our day is short
For these long shadows.'

When I was solemn
You held out laughter, casual as light
For a cigarette.

When I was troubled
Your understanding crossed the bounds of
Words to silence.

When I was frightened
Your eyes said: 'Fear's a child's dream. I too
Have dreamed and woken.'

HOROSCOPE FOR DIANE

Born beneath a troubled star,
Lovelier than others are,
Brighter with the flame of life,
You will cause and suffer strife.

Where you go there will be war;
Where you walk, will walk before
Flattery, and at your back
Envy waiting to attack.

When you look for friends you'll find
Would-be lovers, hungry, blind;
Whom you think you touch and pass,
See! behind you in your glass:

You to whom fate gave the unwise,
Irremediable prize,
Beauty burning, doomed to fire
Too much undesired desire.

LOVE SPEAKS TO THE LOVER

If you'd have rest, take shelter, fly,
For every echo may be I,
At every crack may crouch my spy.

But if unrest, turn from your mirror,
Turn from your dream, to joy, to terror,
Unlearn old wisdom, learn new error.

Stand in your thin skin in my sun
Till skin bears fire and bone's immune
Or skin unflakes and bones melt, run.

Unleash, unfurl. Be sail for wind.
Be seed for prodigal hand to spend.
Cease to plan and begin to be planned.

Be loosed, be used: and I the user.
Be called, be chosen: I the chooser.
Or be refused: I the refuser.

Be pricked by spears, be driven by whips,
Be tortured by doubt's water-drips,
And find strange words upon your lips.

Then, when you've left your harbour-ease
For this light raft wind-caught on these
Unsounded and inconstant seas . . .

Seek, without chart, Hesperides!

SHE

No more time or place
Once I see her face.
Sorrow, doubt and fear
Leave when she is near.
Warm, her eyes and hand,
Wordless, understand.

She, although away,
Stays with me all day,
In, below, behind
Blood and heart and mind.
She is where I go
She is all I know.

Goal and map: to her
I relate, refer
All experience,
Feeling, thought and sense.
Each discovery
Is a prize to be

Shown to her one day:
Something I can lay
Proud before her feet:
Something to repeat:
New-discovered door
We may find once more.

Every day's begun
Charted by her sun.
All I shall not share
Who-knows-when-or-where
With her, and re-taste
By her side, is waste.

II

THE BRITISH

We are a people living in shells and moving
Crablike; reticent, awkward, deeply suspicious;
Watching the world from a corner of half-closed eyelids,
Afraid lest someone show that he hates or loves us,
Afraid lest someone weep in the railway train.

We are coiled and clenched like a fœtus clad in armour.
We hold our hearts for fear they fly like eagles.
We grasp our tongues for fear they cry like trumpets.
We listen to our own footsteps. We look both ways
Before we cross the silent empty road.

We are a people easily made uneasy,
Especially wary of praise, of passion, of scarlet
Cloaks, of gesturing hands, of the smiling stranger
In the alien hat who talks to all or the other
In the unfamiliar coat who talks to none.

We are afraid of too-cold thought or too-hot
Blood, of the opening of long-shut shafts or cupboards,
Of light in caves, of X-rays, probes, unclothing
Of emotion, intolerable revelation
Of lust in the light, of love in the palm of the hand.

We are afraid of, one day on a sunny morning,
Meeting ourselves or another without the usual
Outer sheath, the comfortable conversation,
And saying all, all, all we did not mean to,
All, all, all we did not know we meant.

ENGLAND

(Autumn 1938)

Plush bees above a bed of dahlias;
  Leisurely, timeless garden teas;
Brown bread and honey; scent of mowing;
  The still green light below tall trees.

The ancient custom of deception;
  A Press that seldom stoops to lies—
Merely suppresses truth and twists it,
  Blandly corrupt and slyly wise.

The Common Man; his mask of laughter;
  His back-chat while the roof falls in;
Minorities' long losing battles
  Fought that the sons of sons may win.

The politicians' inward snigger
  (Big Business on the private phone);
The knack of sitting snug on fences;
  The double face of flesh and stone.

Grape-bloom of distant woods at dusk;
  Storm-crown on Glaramara's head;
The fire-rose over London night;
  An old plough rusting autumn-red.

The 'incorruptible policeman'
  Gaoling the whore whose bribe's run out,
Guarding the rich against the poor man,
  Guarding the Settled Gods from doubt.

The generous smile of music-halls,
  Bars and bank-holidays and queues;
The private peace of public foes;
  The truce of pipe and football news.

The smile of privilege exultant;
  Smile at the 'bloody Red' defeated;
Smile at the striker starved and broken;
  Smile at the 'dirty nigger' cheated.

The old hereditary craftsman;
    The incommunicable skill;
The pride in long-loved tools, refusal
    To do the set job quick or ill.

The greater artist mocked, misflattered;
    The lesser forming clique and team
Or crouching in his narrow corner,
    Narcissus with his secret dream.

England of rebels—Blake and Shelley;
    England where freedom's sometimes won,
Where Jew and Negro needn't fear yet
    Lynch-law and pogrom, whip and gun.

England of cant and smug discretion;
    England of wagecut-sweatshop-knight,
Of sportsman-churchman-slum-exploiter,
    Of puritan grown sour with spite.

England of clever fool, mad genius,
    Timorous lion and arrogant sheep,
Half-hearted snob and shamefaced bully,
    Of hands that wake and eyes that sleep . . .
England the snail that's shod with lightning ... .
    Shall we laugh or shall we weep?

POPULAR PRESS

I am the echoing rock that sends you back
Your own voice grown so bold that with surprise
You murmur, 'Ah, how sensible I am—
The plain bluff man, the enemy of sham—
How sane, how wise!'

I am the mirror where your image moves,
Neat and obedient twin, until one day
It moves before you move; and it is you
Who have to ape its moods and motions, who
Must now obey.

LONDON

I and the city of two divided cities
Where the eyes of rich and poor collide and wonder;
Where the beggar's voice is low and unexpectant,
And in clubs the feet of the servants are soft on the carpet
And the world's wind scarcely stirs the leaves of *The Times.*

I am the reticent, the private city,
The city of lovers hiding wrapped in shadows
The city of people sitting and talking quietly
Beyond shut doors and walls as thick as a century,
People who laugh too little and too loudly,
Whose tears fall inward, flowing back to the heart.

I am the city whose fog will fall like a finger gently
Erasing the anger of angles, the strident indecorous gesture,
Whose dusk will come like tact, like a change in the conversation,
Violet and indigo, with strings of lemon streetlamps
Casting their pools into the pools of rain
As the notes of the piano are cast from the top-floor window
Into the square that is always Sunday afternoon.

THE MAN IN THE BOWLER HAT

I am the unnoticed, the unnoticeable man:
The man who sat on your right in the morning train:
The man you looked through like a windowpane:
The man who was the colour of the carriage, the colour of the mounting
Morning pipe-smoke.

I am the man too busy with a living to live,
Too hurried and worried to see and smell and touch:
The man who is patient too long and obeys too much
And wishes too softly and seldom.

I am the man they call the nation's backbone,
Who am boneless – playable catgut, pliable clay:
The Man they label Little lest one day
I dare to grow.

I am the rails on which the moment passes,
The megaphone for many words and voices:
I am graph, diagram,
Composite face.

I am the led, the easily-fed,
The tool, the not-quite-fool,
The would-be-safe-and-sound,
The uncomplaining bound,
The dust fine-ground,
Stone-for-a-statue waveworn pebble-round.

THE AD-MAN

This trumpeter of nothingness, employed
To keep our reason full and null and void:
This man of wind and froth and flux will sell
The wares of any who reward him well,
Praising whatever he is paid to praise,
He hunts for ever-newer, smarter ways
To make the gilt seem gold; the shoddy, silk;
To cheat us legally; to bluff and bilk
By methods which no jury can prevent
Because the law's not broken, only bent.

This mind for hire, this mental prostitute
Can tell the half-lie hardest to refute;
Knows how to hide an inconvenient fact
And when to leave a doubtful claim unbacked;
Manipulates the truth, but not too much,
And if his patter needs the Human Touch
Then aptly artless, artfully naive,
He wears his fickle heart upon his sleeve.

He takes ideas and trains them to engage
In the long little wars big combines wage.
He keeps his logic loose, his feelings flimsy;
Turns eloquence to cant and wit to whimsy;
Trims language till it fits his client's pattern,
And style's a glossy tart or limping slattern.

He uses words that once were strong and fine.
Primal as sun and moon and bread and wine,
True, honourable, honoured, clear and clean,
And leaves them shabby, worn, diminished, mean.

Where our defence is weakest, he attacks.
Encircling reason's fort, he finds the cracks,
He knows the hopes and fears on which to play.
We who at first rebel, at last obey.
We who have tried to choose accept his choice.
Tired, we succumb to his untiring voice.
The drip-drip-drip makes even granite soften.
We trust the brand-name we have heard so often,
And join the queue of sheep that flock to buy:
We fools who know our folly, you and I.

SONG IN A SALOON BAR

We are here for fear we think of
    Things that we would rather not;
We are here lest we remember—
    But we have forgotten what;

Here we need not judge, decipher,
    Justify or understand,
And we fathom nothing deeper
    Than the half-pint in our hand;

Here we turn from shadows' questions—
    Who we have been, will be, are—
To the comfortable voices
    Telling stories in the bar;

Here we turn from ghosts and, turning,
    Turn the amber, honey-bright,
Frosted-gold or copper-tawny
    Glassful in the smoky light;

Somewhere yesterday-tomorrow's
    Closing like two closing claws,
But, in here, each mild-and-bitter
    Makes the cunning clock-hands pause;

Let us cluster and stand closer
    Lest we've room to turn and run;
Time for one more round, old man, for . . .
    Time for, time for . . . one, for one . . .

We are here for fear we think of
    Things that we would rather not;
We are here lest we remember —
    But we have forgotten what.

MONEY TALKS

Money talks with a voice that's thinned
To a rustle of chequebooks in the wind.

Money talks with a voice as dry
As an auditor's enquiring eye.

Money talks with a voice that clanks
Like slamming doors of closing banks.

Money talks with the hollow sound
Of metal boxes underground.

' Inflation's floods are dark and drear.
The deserts of deflation sear.

My enemies are always near.'
Money talks with a voice of fear.

EPILOGUE

I am proud, humble, stupid, clever, anonymous
Man, who am lost in the only world I know;
Blind in my mask and tripped by my disguises;
Used by my tools and wounded by my weapons;
Chased by my echo, scared by my long shadow;
Fumbling with delicate hands; longing to be
Myself (who who? but who? if I only knew!);
Groping; self-torn, self-tortured, self-condemned;
Wormeaten angel, welter of dust and flame.

A MAN OF CULTURE

He finds that that talk of music, books and art is
Useful at all the most important parties.
He cultivates an aptitude for knowing
Which way the day's aesthetic wind is blowing.
He lacks all passion, feels no love or hate;
Notes what is up to, what is out of, date;
Is equally prepared to praise or damn
So long as he can coin an epigram.
Spying the coming man before he's come,
He beats the first premonitory drum;
Aware which reputation's almost dead,
He plans the funeral speech a year ahead.
His seismographic needle will betray
A falling fashion half the world away;
Yet good and bad in art are one to him,
Mirror of mode and weathercock of whim.

Established in his eminence of taste,
This little man has little time to waste:
And so the only books at which he looks
Are books on books, or books on books on books.
He shines, but shines with cold reflected light,
Bold without risk, derivatively right,
Lame but for crutches, but for prompters dumb,
Index of others, every summary's sum.
Rich by much robbing, smart at second hand,
Builder with borrowed bricks on shifting sand,
Reaper of fields dug deep by earlier spades,
Echo of echoes, shadower of shades.

MASTER OF HYPOCHONDRIA

How happily you sit among a host of
Cures to part-cure the ills you make the most of:
You who are many doctors, many patients
Rolled into one; who plan your permutations
With tranquilliser counteracting tonic,
Stimulant, sedative : Napoleonic
Maestro of civil war : Bach with a theme
As long as life, as lovely as a dream!

Expert in analgesics, trained in taking
Aspirin soon enough to end the aching
Anti-biotics often leave behind them,
You master pains with pains and do not mind them.

Teach me your alchemy! I'll plumb and ponder
Psychosomatic mysteries. I'll wander
Deep in your maze. I'll learn from you to study
My graph, my chart, head neither bowed nor bloody.
We'll meet in Samarkand, the golden city
Of all who play the trumpets of self-pity,
Whose hearts lament like violins above
The thunder-roll of drums men call self-love.

AGE

Do men grow wholly old;
Unknowing, tire of living;
Grow deaf as pulse grows faint;
Dream and in dreams depart?

Or do they wake, feel cold
And hear – a salt sea grieving
In landlocked, long complaint –
The all-too-youthful heart?

THE PSYCHIATRIST SPEAKS

Quietly, patiently I wait
(And sometimes gently probe and peer)
To find the love, the lust, the hate,
The wound, the mystery, the fear
Within the mind-within-the-mind;
The mind that's like a face behind
A window-curtain seeing unseen,
The mind that's wiser than you know,
The mind that says the things you mean,
The mind that's swift when you are slow,
The mind that wakes when daylight mind
Sleeps – and that sees when the other's blind;
The mind that seems to lie so still
But moves calm-surely to its goal
As compass-needle moves to pole.

And then – when I (or rather you)
Have found the last and deepest clue,
The hate you hate, the fear you fear,
The worm that lies beneath the stone,
The ghost in that one room alone
Whose door you never dare unlock,
The secret you've forgotten so
Successfully so long ago
(And yet it's in that ticking clock,
It's on your track behind your back,
Slowly, invisibly drawing near,
Softly preparing to attack) –
Then I say, 'Learn at last to live
Without your sackcloth, to forgive
Yourself the innocent sin, to cast
The burden of guilt away at last!'

THE NEUROTICS

We are the double people, goaled and goaler,
Sparrow and hawk in one uneasy body;
We are a battlefield but cannot clearly
Remember why the fight or when it started.

We are the builders of small doorless houses,
Walls to defy the other world which always
Peers in at us through widening cracks that vainly
We cram with mud or paper or our fingers.

Some of us build our secret world by gathering
Fans or old playing cards or Balkan watches
To hoard and pattern, love and list and label:
Kingdom in which we're king and none may enter.

Some of us build our world with pornographic
Postcards or drugs or mistresses or money,
Private religions or a cipher diary
Or great inventions in an attic drawer.

Some of us spend our lives preventing others
From doing what we cannot or we dare not,
And stand in shadow spitting at the sunlight,
And watch at keyholes for the Day of Judgment.

Some of us play at games with blood and nightmares,
Pricking a tender nerve with mental needles,
Twisting a mind as schoolboys twist a forearm,
Pinning the human fly beneath the tumbler.

Some of us populate our days and nights with
Enemies laying plots to trip or maim us,
To make us halt by roofs when tiles are falling
Or lose umbrellas, chances, buses, lovers.

Some of us wander reaching, reaching, reaching
Backwards in time as down into dark water
To find the clockwork mouse that broke, the woolly
Bear that we lost among the tall black fir-trees.

We are the dwellers in the middle limbo,
Land that we hate yet land that holds our landmarks,
Land where we cannot rest yet stay unresting.
Land that we long to leave but fear to start from.

We are the walkers in eternal circles
To whom the circle's better than its breaking,
To whom unhappiness has long grown easier
Than happiness; to whom this twilight's home.

THE PSYCHO-ANALYST

His suit is good, his hands are white.
He smiles all day, and sleeps all night
Because he's always, always right.

He states his theory. You agree?
Well then, of course, it's plain to see
That he is right as right can be!

You disagree? Ah, that is mere
Resistance to the facts you fear:
Truth is confirmed, the case is clear!

So you are free as air to choose,
Take his advice or spurn his views,
But heads he wins and tails you lose.

His fees are large, his cares are light,
His analytic eyes are bright,
He glows with pride as well he might.

The analyst is always right.

PORTRAIT OF A ROMANTIC

He is in love with the land that is always over
The next hill and the next, with the bird that is never
Caught, with the room beyond the looking-glass.

He likes the half-hid, the half-heard, the half-lit,
The man in the fog, the road without an ending,
Stray pieces of torn words to piece together.

He is well aware that man is always lonely,
Listening for an echo of his cry, crying for the moon,
Making the moon his mirror, weeping in the night.

He often dives in the deep-sea undertow
Of the dark and dreaming mind. He turns at corners,
Twists on his heel to trap his following shadow.

He is haunted by the face behind the face.
He searches for last frontiers and lost doors.
He tries to climb the wall around the world.

III

SLEEP

The ring and rim
Of tidal sleep
Will slip and creep
Along my limbs

And I shall watch,
But never catch
The final change,
The water-plunge,

And through what caves
Beneath what waves
I then shall go
I shall not know

For I shall come
From that lost land
Half-blind, half-dumb,
With, in my hand,

A fish's head,
A shell, a shred
Of seaweed and
Some grains of sand.

CATS

I

To walk as you walk, green eye, smiler, not
Even ostentatiously alone but simply
Alone . . . arching the back in courteous discourtesy,
Gathering the body as a dancer before an unworthy
Audience, treading earth scantly—a task to be done
And done with, girt (curt introvert) for private
Precise avoidance of the undesired,
Pride-attired, generalissimo
Knife-eyed, bisector of moonshine with indigo
Shadow, scorner of earth-floor, flaunter of
Steel-hard sickle curve against the sky . . . !

II

Cats, no less liquid than their shadows,
    Offer no angles to the wind.
They slip, diminished, neat, through loopholes
    Less than themselves; will not be pinned

To rules or routes for journeys; counter
    Attack with non-resistance; twist
Enticing through the curving fingers
    And leave an angered, empty fist.

They wait, obsequious as darkness—.
    Quick to retire, quick to return;
Admit no aim or ethics; flatter
    With reservations; will not learn

To answer to their names; are seldom
    Truly owned till shot and skinned.
Cats, no less liquid than their shadows,
    Offer no angles to the wind.

NIGHT-LIFE

The useful and domestic cat
Adorning the familial mat,
Now at the fall of purple dusk,
Suffers a change. He sheds the husk
Of civilisation, and returns
To his primeval self. He burns
With atavistic nomadry,
And yearns to be abroad and free;
Nor longer loves the household lars,
But only seeks the cruel stars . . .
Now he is in the pallid gleam
His fur unsleeks, his features seem
To assume a diabolic leer,
His eyes expand, he cocks an ear:
And all the urbanity of day
Turns to an ardent lust for prey . . .
But when comes dawn, with slaked desire,
He sits again before the fire.

DISCOVERY

When you are slightly drunk
Things are so close, so friendly.
The road asks to be walked upon,
The road rewards you for walking
With firm upward contact answering your downward
    contact
Like the pressure of a hand in yours.
You think—this studious balancing
Of right leg while left leg advances, of left while right,
How splendid
Like somebody-or-other-on-a-peak-in-Darien!
How cleverly that seat shapes the body of the girl
    who sits there.
How well, how skilfully that man there walks to-
    wards you,
Arms hanging, swinging, waiting.
You move the muscles of your cheeks,
How cunningly a smile responds.
And now you are actually speaking
Round sounding words
Magnificent
As that lady's hat!

EDITH PIAF

Voice of one whose heart
    Has mended with the years,
One who can stand apart
    And laugh at life through tears.

Voice of one who has long
    Outlived regret, outgrown
Hope, and at last is strong
    Enough to stand alone.

WET CITY NIGHT

Light drunkenly reels into shadow;
Blurs, slurs uneasily;
Slides off the eyeballs:
The segments shatter.

Tree-branches cut arc-light in ragged
Fluttering wet strips.
The cup of the sky-sign is filled too full;
It slushes wine over.

The street-lamps dance a tarantella
And zigzag down the street:
They lift and fly away
In a wind of lights.

A HOT DAY

Cottonwool clouds loiter.
A lawnmower, very far,
Birrs. Then a bee comes
To a crimson rose and softly,
Deftly and fatly crams
A velvet body in.

A tree, June-lazy, makes
A tent of dim green light.
Sunlight weaves in the leaves,
Honey-light laced with leaf-light,
Green interleaved with gold.
Sunlight gathers its rays
In sheaves, which the wind unweaves
And then reweaves—the wind
That puffs a smell of grass
Through the heat-heavy, trembling
Summer pool of air.

JAMAICAN BUS RIDE

The live fowl squatting on the grapefruit and bananas
in the basket of the copper-coloured lady
is gloomy but resigned.
The four very large baskets on the floor
are in everybody's way,
as the conductor points out
loudly, often, but in vain.

Two quadroon dandies are disputing
who is standing on whose feet.

When we stop,
a boy vanishes through the door marked ENTRANCE;
but those entering through the door marked EXIT
are greatly hindered by the fact that when we started
there were twenty standing,
and another ten have somehow inserted themselves
into invisible crannies
between dark sweating body and body.

With an odour of petrol
both excessive and alarming
we hurtle hell-for-leather
between crimson bougainvillea blossom
and scarlet poinsettia
and miraculously do not run over
three goats, seven hens and a donkey
as we pray
that the driver has not fortified himself
at Daisy's Drinking Saloon
with more than four rums:
or by the gods of Jamaica
this day is our last!

THE IMPLACABLE STREETS

On certain afternoons
The streets start to repeat
Themselves and after the corner
The faces at the windows
Are the same and the gulf between
The walls is very tall
And houses suddenly lean
Closer and there's no clue
And everyone you meet
Is lost without retreat
And each one hunts in vain
For an unknown address
And all begins again.

SUMMER NIGHT AT HYDE PARK CORNER

Great globes of light spill yellow rain:
    Pencils of gold through purple gloom.
The buses swarm like heavy bees
    Trailing fat bodies. Faces loom,
Moonlike, and fade away among the trees
    Which, lit beneath by lamplight, bloom
High in darkness. Distant traffic
    Sounds with dull, enclosing boom . . .

Sleep extends a velvet forepaw.
    Night spreads out a downsoft plume.

CHAPLIN

The sun, a heavy spider, spins in the thirsty sky.
The wind hides under cactus leaves, in doorway
corners. Only the wry

Small shadow accompanies Hamlet-Petrouchka's
march—the slight
Wry sniggering shadow in front in the morning,
turning at noon, behind towards night.

The plumed cavalcade has passed to to-morrow, is
lost again;
But the wisecrack-mask, the quick-flick-fanfare of the
cane remain.

Diminuendo of footsteps even is done:
Only remain, Don Quixote, hat, cane, smile and sun.

Goliaths fall to our sling, but craftier fates than these
Lie ambushed—malice of open manholes, strings in
the dark and falling trees.

God kicks our backsides, scatters peel on the
smoothest stair;
And towering centaurs steal the tulip lips, the
aureoled hair,

While we, craned from the gallery, throw our card-
board flowers
And our feet jerk to tunes not played for ours.

FLIGHT OF STAIRS

Stairs fly as straight as hawks;
Or else in spirals, curve out of curve, pausing
At a ledge to poise their wings before relaunching.
Stairs sway at the height of their flight
Like a melody in Tristan;
Or swoop to the ground with glad spread of their
        feathers
Before they close them.

They curiously investigate
The shells of buildings,
A hollow core,
Shell in a shell.

Useless to produce their path to infinity
Or turn it to a moral symbol,
For their flight is ambiguous, upwards or downwards
        as you please;
Their fountain is frozen,
Their concertina is silent.

BELLS, POOL AND SLEEP

Bells overbrim with sound
And spread from cupolas
Out through the shaking air
Endless unbreaking circles
Cool and clear as water.

A stone dropped in the water
Opens the lips of the pool
And starts the unovertaking
Rings, till the pool is full
Of waves as the air of bells.

The deep-sea bell of sleep
Under the pool of the mind
Flowers in concentric circles
Of annihilation till
Both sight and sound die out,
Both pool and bells are quelled.

EARTHFAST

Architects plant their imagination, weld their
 poems on rock,
Clamp them to the skidding rim of the world and
 anchor them down to its core;
Leave more than the painter's or poet's snail-bright
 trail on a friable leaf;
Can build their chrysalis round them—stand in their
 sculpture's belly.

They see through stone, they cage and partition air,
 they cross-rig space
With footholds, planks for a dance; yet their maze,
 their flying trapeze
Is pinned to the centre. They write their euclidean
 music standing
With a hand on a cornice of cloud, themselves set
 fast, earth-square.

LA MARCHE DES MACHINES

This piston's infinite recurrence is
night morning night and morning night and
death and birth and death and birth and this
crank climbs (blind Sisyphus) and see

steel teeth greet
bow deliberate
delicately lace
in lethal kiss
        God's teeth bite whitely tight

slowly the gigantic oh slowly the steel spine dislocates

wheels grazing (accurately missing) waltz

two cranes do a hundred-ton tango against the sky.

(*Suggested by Deslav's film of the same title*)

IN CANTERBURY CATHEDRAL

Trees, but straighter than birches, rise to the sky
Of stone. Their branches meet in the sky of stone.
Stone fountains leap and meet: their traceries are
As light as lace. These prayers of stone were prayed
To a God I can't believe in, but were made
By Man, men almost gods, in whom I can
Believe: were made as strong, to last as long
As time. I stare and pray to Man alone.

SKATERS' WALTZ

'. . . So tempting to let freeze
    One's deepest, darkest pools
And learn to skim with ease
    Thin ice; for who but fools

Dive into who-knows-what?'
    'But if the ice by chance
Breaks?' 'But if not, if not?
    And how it glitters! Dance!'

ONE ALMOST MIGHT

Wouldn't you say,
Wouldn't you say: one day,
With a little more time or a little more patience, one
    might
Disentangle for separate, deliberate, slow delight
One of the moment's hundred strands, unfray
Beginnings from endings, this from that, survey
Say a square inch of the ground one stands on, touch
Part of oneself or a leaf or a sound (not clutch
Or cuff or bruise but touch with finger-tip, ear-
Tip, eyetip, creeping near yet not too near);
Might take up life and lay it on one's palm
And, encircling it in closeness, warmth and calm,
Let it lie still, then stir smooth-softly, and
Tendril by tendril unfold, there on one's hand . . .

One might examine eternity's cross-section
For a second, with slightly more patience, more time
    for reflection?

DEAF ANIMAL

Man can talk, but seldom
Listen; for he hears
Less the words that are spoken
Than his own hopes and fears.

Man can be taught perhaps only
That which he almost knows
For only in soil that is ready
Grows the mind's obstinate rose.

The right word at the wrong time
Is wind-caught, blown away;
And the most that the ages' sages'
Wisdom and wit can say

Is no more to the quickest pupil
Than a midwife's delicate steady
Fingers aiding and easing
The thought half-born already.

And argument is either
A game light as a smile
Where the players' equal cheating
Observes the laws of guile,

Or a bitter and bleeding duel
Fought by the angry and blind
(But tomorrow the loser will vanquish
The victor's ghost in his mind).

And all the comforter's eager
Awkward speech is only
A song-without-words whose tune will
Lull, for a while, the lonely.

FOOTNOTES ON HAPPINESS

Happiness filters
Out through a crack in the door, through the net's
        reticulations.
But also in.

The old cat Patience
Watching the hole with folded paws and quiet tail
Can seldom catch it.

Timetables fail.
It rarely stands at a certain moment a certain day
At a certain bus-stop.

You cannot say
It will keep an appointment, or pass the same street corner
        twice.
Nor say it won't.

Lavender, ice,
Camphor, glass cases, vacuum chambers hermetically
        sealed,
Won't keep it fresh.

It will not yield
Except to the light, the careless, the accidental hand,
And easily bruises.

It is brittle as sand.
It is more and less than you hoped to find. It has never
        quite
Your own ideas.

It shows no spite
Or favour in choosing its host. It is, like God,
Casual, odd.

NURSERY RHYME FOR A TWENTY-FIRST BIRTHDAY

You cannot see the walls that divide your hand
From his or hers or mine when you think you touch it.

You cannot see the walls because they are glass,
And glass is nothing until you try to pass it.

Beat on it if you like, but not too hard,
For glass will break you even while you break it.

Shout, and the sound will be broken, and driven
        backwards,
For glass, though clear as water, is deaf as granite.

This fraudulent inhibition is cunning: wise men
Content themselves with breathing patterns on it.

INVITATION TO THE DANCE

Enough, my brain, of these circles, circles.
        Cease, caged enemy, cease.
Others have thought these thoughts before you.
        Peace, brain; peace.

It has all been written in books, and better.
        Come, let the tidal sweep
Of the music run through our veins' slow delta.
        (Sleep, brain; sleep).

Music will rise in us, rise like the dance of
        Growth; like sap's long riot.
Limbs understand. Thighs have their language.
    (Quiet, brain; quiet.)

Listen. This tune is a sea, resolving
        Crest upon breaking crest.
Feet weave a web that unweaves behind us.
    Rest, brain; rest. Rest.

MEETING

Dogs take new friends abruptly and by smell.
Cats' meetings are neat, tactual, caressive.
Monkeys exchange their fleas before they speak.
Snakes, no doubt, coil by coil reach mutual know-
        ledge.

We then, at first encounter, should be silent;
Not court the cortex but the epidermis;
Not work from inside out but outside in;
Discover each other's flesh, its scent and texture;
Familiarize the sinews and the nerve-ends,
The hands, the hair – before the inept lips open.

Instead of which we are resonant, explicit.
Our words like windows intercept our meaning.
Our four eyes fence and flinch and awkwardly
Wince into shadow, slide oblique to ambush.
Hands stir, retract. The pulse is insulated.
Blood is turned inwards, lonely; skin unhappy . . .
While always under all, but interrupted,
Antennæ stretch . . . waver . . . and almost . . . touch.

TALK IN THE NIGHT

'Why are you sighing?'
        'For all the voyages I did not make
        Because the boat was small, might leak, might take
        The wrong course, and the compass might be broken,
        And I might have awoken
        In some strange sea and heard
        Strange birds crying.'

'Why are you weeping?'
        'For all the unknown friends or lovers passed
        Because I watched the ground or walked too fast
        Or simply did not see
        Or turned aside for tea
        For fear an old wound stirred
        From its sleeping.'

IF MEN WERE NOT STRIPED LIKE TIGERS

How much simpler if men were not striped like tigers,
 patched like clowns;
If alternate white and black were not further confused by
 greys and browns;
If people were, even at times, consistent wholes;
If the actors were rigidly typed and kept their roles;
If we were able
To classify friends, each with his label,
Each label neat
As the names of cakes or the categories of meat.
But you, my dear, are a greedy bitch, yet also a sad child
 lost,
And you who have swindled your partners are kind to
 the cat,
And, in human beings, this is not this nor that quite that
And the threads are crossed
And nothing's as tidy as the mind could wish
And the human mammal is partly insect and often reptile
 and also fish.

FATE WRITE TWO EPITAPHS

1. On Any Man

I let him find, but never what he sought;
 I let him act, but never as he meant;
And, after much mislearning, he was taught,
 Tired, to be content with discontent.

2. On Man

He had great virtues, but a seed of terror
 Corrupted him; fear made him cruel, mean;
So I repealed an all-but glorious error,
 Wiped off a little dust, and left earth clean.

SAVING GRACE

Fish do not smile, nor birds: their faces are not
Equipped for it. A smiling dog's the illusion
And wish-fulfilment of its owner. Cats wear
Permanent smiles inspired by mere politeness.
But human animals at times forget their
Godlike responsibilities; the tension
Slackens, the weasel-sharp intentness falters;
Muscles relax; the eyes refrain from peering
Aside, before and after; and the burden
Of detail drops from forehead; cheekline gently
Creases; the mouth wide-flowers; the stiff mask softens;
And Man bestows his simple, unambitious,
Unservile, unselfseeking, undeceptive,
Uncorrupt gift, the grace-note of a smile.

LAST WORD TO CHILDHOOD

Ice-cold fear has slowly decreased
As my bones have grown, my height increased.
Though I shiver in snow of dreams, I shall never
Freeze again in a noonday terror.

I shall never break, my sinews crumble
As God-the-headmaster's fingers fumble
At the other side of unopening doors
Which I watch for a hundred thousand years.

I shall never feel my thin blood leak
While darkness stretches a paw to strike
Or Nothing beats an approaching drum
Behind my back in a silent room.

I shall never, alone, meet the end of my world
At the bend of a path, the turn of a wall:
Never, or once more only, and
That will be once, and an end of end.

DAYDREAM

One day people will touch and talk perhaps easily,
And loving be natural as breathing and warm as sunlight,
And people will untie themselves, as string is unknotted,
Unfold and yawn and stretch and spread their fingers,
Unfurl, uncurl like seaweed returned to the sea,
And work will be simple and swift as a seagull flying,
And play will be casual and quiet as a seagull settling,
And the clocks will stop, and no-one will wonder or
        care or notice,
And people will smile without reason, even in the winter,
        even in the rain.

EPITAPH FOR OUR CHILDREN

Blame us for these who were cradled and rocked in our chaos
    Watching our sidelong watching, fearing our fear;
Playing their blindman's buff in our gutted mansions,
    Their follow-my-leader on a stair that ended in air.

HEAVEN

In the heaven of the god I hope for (call him X)
There is marriage and giving in marriage and transient sex
For those who will cast the body's vest aside
Soon, but are not yet wholly rarified
And still embrace. For X is never annoyed
Or shocked; has read his Jung and knows his Freud,
He gives you time in heaven to do as you please,
To climb love's gradual ladder by slow degrees,
Gently to rise from sense to soul, to ascend
To a world of timeless joy, world without end.

Here on the gates of pearl there hangs no sign
Limiting cakes and ale, forbidding wine.
No weakness here is hidden, no vice unknown.
Sin is a sickness to be cured, outgrown.
With the help of a god who can laugh, an unsolemn god
Who smiles at old wives' tales of iron rod
And fiery hell, a god who's more at ease
With bawds and Falstaffs than with pharisees.

Here the lame learn to leap, the blind to see.
Tyrants are taught to be humble, slaves to be free.
Fools become wise, and wise men cease to be bores,
Here bishops learn from lips of back-street whores,
And white men follow black-faced angels' feet
Through fields of orient and immortal wheat.

Villon, Lautrec and Baudelaire are here.
Here Swift forgets his anger, Poe his fear.
Napoleon rests. Columbus, journeys done,
Has reached his new Atlantis, found his sun.
Verlaine and Dylan Thomas drink together.
Marx talks to Plato. Byron wonders whether
There's some mistake. Wordsworth has found a hill
That's home. Here Chopin plays the piano still.
Wren plans ethereal domes; and Renoir paints
Young girls as ripe as fruit but not yet saints.

And X, of whom no coward is afraid,
Who's friend consulted, not fierce king obeyed;
Who hears the unspoken thought, the prayer unprayed;
Who expects not even the learned to understand
His universe, extends a prodigal hand,
Full of forgiveness, over his promised land.